CAPYBARAS
Photos and Facts for Everyone

Animals in Nature

By Isis Gaillard

Learn With Facts Series

Book 137

Image Credits: Royalty-free images reproduced under license from various stock image repositories.

Isis Gaillard. Capybaras Photos and Facts for Everyone Animals in Nature Learn With Pictures Series Book 137.

Learn With Facts an imprint of TLM Media LLC

ISBN-13: 979-8-88700-657-4

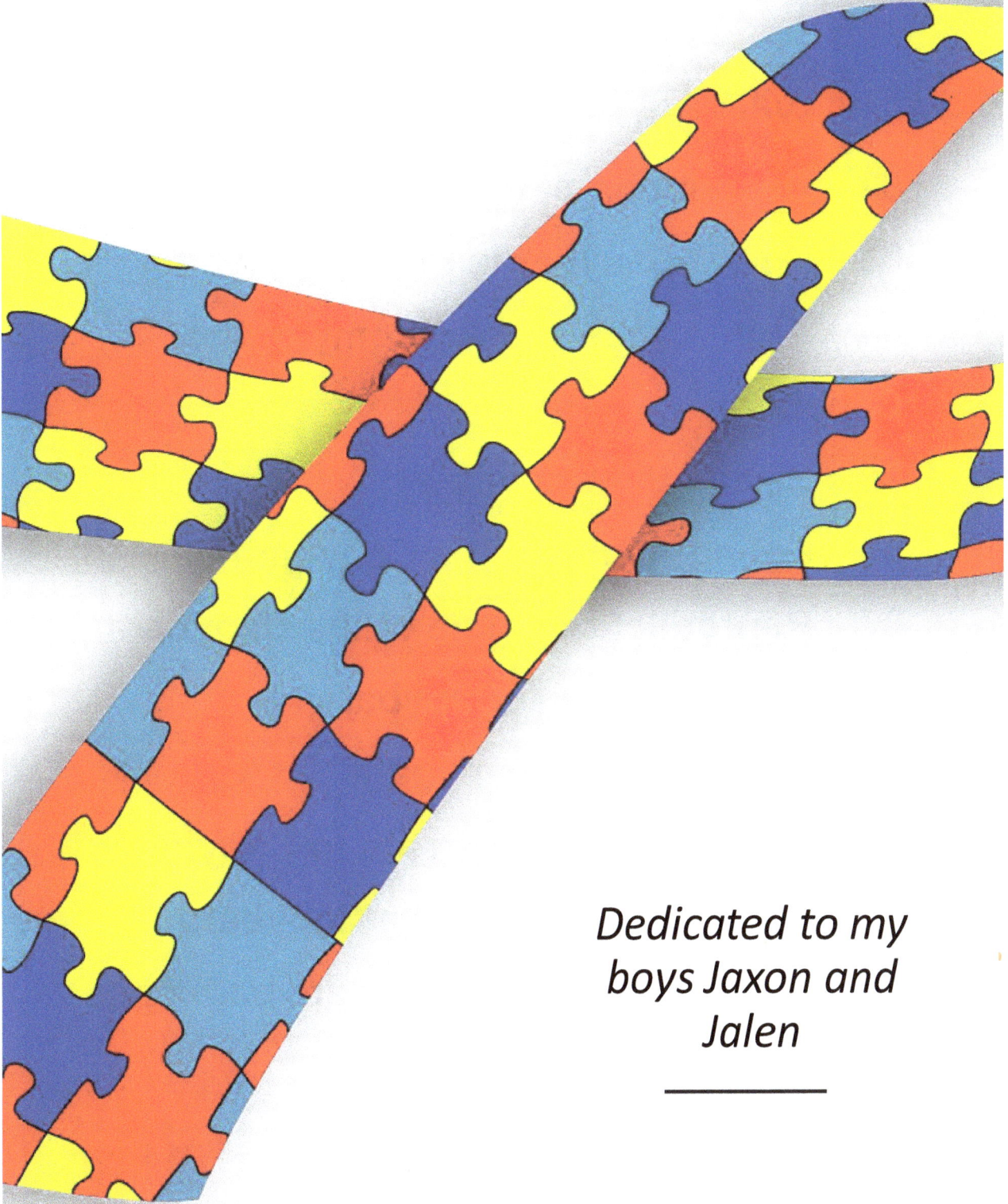

Dedicated to my boys Jaxon and Jalen

———

Table of Contents

1. What Is a Capybara? – Introduction

The capybara is the largest living rodent in the world and is known for its calm nature, strong social bonds, and close connection to water. Native to South America, the capybara is a semi-aquatic mammal that thrives in environments where land and water meet. Its unique combination of size, behavior, and adaptability makes it one of the most fascinating mammals on Earth.

Capybaras belong to the rodent family, which also includes animals such as mice, rats, squirrels, and guinea pigs. Despite this classification, capybaras are much larger and differ significantly in behavior and appearance from smaller rodents. Their bodies are built for both land movement and swimming, allowing them to move easily between grassy areas and water sources.

One of the defining characteristics of capybaras is their strong dependence on water. They spend a large portion of their lives near rivers, lakes, marshes, and wetlands. Water provides protection from predators, helps regulate body temperature, and plays a role in social interaction. Capybaras are excellent swimmers and can remain submerged for several minutes when escaping danger.

Capybaras are herbivores, feeding mainly on grasses and aquatic plants. Their diet and digestive system are adapted to extract nutrients from tough plant material. This feeding strategy allows them to thrive in environments where plant life is abundant but predators are also common.

Social behavior is a key part of capybara life. Unlike many rodents that live alone, capybaras form large, organized groups. These groups provide protection, improve survival, and help raise young. Their calm temperament and tolerance of other animals have earned them a reputation as one of the most peaceful mammals in the animal kingdom.

Culturally, capybaras have been part of human life in South America for centuries. They appear in local traditions, agriculture, and modern media. In recent years,

capybaras have gained global popularity due to their relaxed behavior and unique appearance.

Ecologically, capybaras play an important role in maintaining healthy ecosystems. By grazing on grasses and aquatic plants, they help shape vegetation growth and support biodiversity. They also serve as prey for large predators, making them an essential link in the food chain.

Overall, the capybara is more than just a large rodent. It is a highly adapted mammal whose physical traits, social structure, and lifestyle allow it to survive successfully in complex environments. Its balance of strength, calmness, and adaptability makes it one of nature's most remarkable animals.

2. Description of the Capybara

The capybara has a distinctive appearance that reflects its semi-aquatic lifestyle and social nature. As the largest rodent in the world, its body is built for strength, stability, and endurance rather than speed. Every physical feature of the capybara supports life in wetlands, grasslands, and water-rich environments.

Capybaras have large, barrel-shaped bodies covered in coarse, short fur. Their fur is typically brown, reddish-brown, or grayish in color, which helps them blend into grassy fields, muddy riverbanks, and marshy surroundings. This natural camouflage reduces visibility to predators and provides protection while resting or grazing.

The head of a capybara is broad and blunt, with a square-shaped muzzle. Their eyes, ears, and nostrils are positioned high on the head. This placement allows capybaras to keep most of their body submerged in water while still seeing, hearing, and breathing. This adaptation is especially important for avoiding predators, as capybaras can remain almost completely hidden while monitoring their surroundings.

Capybaras have small, rounded ears that are highly sensitive to sound. Their hearing helps them detect predators even in dense vegetation. The eyes are dark and expressive, offering good vision both on land and near the water's surface. While their eyesight is not specialized for detail, it is effective for detecting movement.

The mouth of a capybara contains large, strong front teeth called incisors. Like all rodents, these teeth grow continuously throughout life. Capybaras constantly gnaw on grasses and plants, which helps keep their teeth worn down to a healthy length. Behind the incisors are flat molars used to grind tough plant material.

Their neck is short and thick, blending smoothly into the body. This reduces drag while swimming and adds strength when pushing through vegetation. The chest and shoulders are powerful, supporting movement on land and stability in water.

Capybaras have four short but sturdy legs. Their front legs are slightly shorter than their hind legs, giving them a forward-leaning posture. Each foot has partially webbed toes, an important adaptation for swimming. The webbing helps propel the capybara through water and provides traction on muddy or slippery surfaces.

Unlike many mammals, capybaras have almost no visible tail. This lack of a tail reduces drag while swimming and prevents injury in dense vegetation. Their streamlined shape makes it easier to move between land and water without obstruction.

The skin of a capybara is thick and tough, providing protection from scratches, bites, and environmental exposure. This durable skin also helps prevent injury during conflicts with predators or while moving through rough terrain.

Internally, capybaras have a highly specialized digestive system designed to process fibrous plant material. Their large stomach and complex intestines allow them to extract nutrients from grasses that many other animals cannot digest efficiently. This internal structure supports their herbivorous lifestyle and allows them to spend many hours grazing each day.

Overall, the physical description of the capybara reveals an animal perfectly adapted for a life of calm movement, social living, and close connection to water. Its size, body structure, and sensory adaptations allow it to thrive in challenging environments while maintaining a peaceful and cooperative lifestyle.

3. Where Capybaras Live and Habitat

Capybaras are native to **South America** and are closely tied to environments where land and water exist side by side. Their survival depends on access to fresh water, open grazing areas, and dense vegetation for shelter. Because of this strong dependency, capybaras are considered **semi-aquatic mammals**, spending much of their lives moving between water and land.

Countries with wild capybaras

Countries with zoos with capybaras

Countries with both wild and zoo capybaras

Created with mapchart.net

Geographic Range

Capybaras are found across a wide portion of South America, including regions with warm climates and abundant freshwater systems. Their range extends through areas where rivers, lakes, wetlands, and floodplains are common. These environments provide the essential resources capybaras need for feeding, protection, and social living.

They are especially common in lowland regions where seasonal flooding creates rich grasslands and shallow water bodies. These conditions support large groups and allow capybaras to thrive in stable populations.

Preferred Habitat Types

Capybaras live in a variety of habitats, but all share one key feature: **access to water**. Common habitats include:

Riverbanks
Marshes and swamps
Flooded grasslands
Lakeshores
Wet savannas

Water is essential not only for drinking but also for cooling the body, escaping predators, mating, and resting. Capybaras often enter the water multiple times a day.

Role of Water in Daily Life

Capybaras are excellent swimmers and use water as their primary defense mechanism. When threatened, they quickly retreat into rivers or lakes, where they can swim efficiently or remain submerged with only their eyes and nostrils visible.

Water also helps regulate body temperature. In hot climates, capybaras spend long periods soaking to avoid overheating. Muddy water can also protect their skin from sun exposure and insects.

Vegetation and Shelter

Dense vegetation near water sources is crucial for capybaras. Tall grasses, reeds, and shrubs provide:

Cover from predators

Shade from the sun
Safe resting areas for young

Capybaras typically graze in open areas during early morning or late afternoon, then retreat into thicker vegetation during the hottest parts of the day.

Seasonal Habitat Changes

Capybaras adapt well to seasonal changes. During rainy seasons, when large areas flood, they spread out across newly available land and water. During dry seasons, they gather near remaining water sources, sometimes forming very large groups.

These seasonal movements help them survive environmental changes but can also increase competition for food and space during droughts.

Human-Modified Environments

Capybaras are highly adaptable and can live near human settlements if conditions are suitable. They are sometimes found near:

Agricultural lands
Irrigation canals
Artificial lakes and reservoirs

While these environments can provide food and water, they also expose capybaras to risks such as vehicle traffic, hunting, and habitat conflict with humans.

Habitat Importance to Survival

The availability and quality of habitat directly affect capybara health and population size. Loss of wetlands, water pollution, and land development can reduce suitable living space. Without access to clean water and grazing areas, capybaras struggle to survive.

Protecting capybara habitats also benefits many other species, as wetlands support high biodiversity and healthy ecosystems.

Why Habitat Defines the Capybara

Capybaras are not just animals that live near water — their entire biology, behavior, and social structure are shaped by it. Their habitat determines:

Group size
Feeding patterns
Predator avoidance
Reproductive success

This strong connection makes the capybara a powerful example of how animals evolve in harmony with their environment.

4. Appearance and Anatomy of the Capybara

The appearance and anatomy of the capybara reflect a mammal that is perfectly adapted to a semi-aquatic lifestyle, social living, and constant grazing. Every physical feature of the capybara supports movement between land and water while allowing it to survive in environments filled with predators and environmental challenges.

Overall Body Structure

Capybaras have large, heavy, barrel-shaped bodies that give them stability rather than speed. Their bodies are long and thick, with a low center of gravity that helps them remain balanced while walking on muddy ground or swimming through water. This body shape allows them to rest comfortably on land and float easily in water.

Their build is solid and muscular, especially around the shoulders and hindquarters. This strength supports long periods of walking, swimming, and standing while grazing.

Head, Eyes, Ears, and Nose Placement

One of the most important anatomical adaptations of the capybara is the placement of its facial features. The eyes, ears, and nostrils are all positioned high on the head. This allows the capybara to keep most of its body submerged while still being able to see, hear, and breathe.

This feature is crucial for predator avoidance. When danger approaches, a capybara can quietly enter the water and remain nearly invisible, exposing only the top of its head above the surface.

Eyes and Vision

Capybara eyes are dark and slightly protruding, giving them a wide field of vision. While their eyesight is not designed for sharp detail, it is excellent at detecting

movement. This helps capybaras notice predators approaching from a distance, especially in open grasslands.

Their eyes are also adapted to function near water, allowing them to see reasonably well while swimming or resting at the water's edge.

Ears and Hearing

Capybaras have small, rounded ears that can rotate slightly to capture sounds from different directions. Their hearing is highly developed and plays a major role in group communication and predator detection.

In social groups, capybaras rely on sound to stay alert. Alarm calls, whistles, and barks warn others of danger and help coordinate group movement.

Teeth and Jaw Structure As rodents, capybaras have large, powerful incisors that grow continuously throughout their lives. These front teeth are sharp and strong, allowing them to cut through tough grasses and plants. Behind the incisors are broad molars used for grinding food into digestible material.

Constant grazing naturally wears down the teeth, preventing overgrowth. This dental structure is essential for survival, as improper tooth wear can lead to serious health problems.

Limbs and Feet

Capybaras have four short but sturdy legs. Their legs are well suited for walking long distances and supporting their heavy bodies. The front legs are slightly shorter than the hind legs, giving them a forward-leaning posture.

Each foot has **partially webbed toes**, an important adaptation for swimming. The webbing increases surface area, allowing capybaras to paddle efficiently through water and maintain balance on muddy or slippery surfaces.

Skin and Fur

Capybara fur is coarse, sparse, and short. It is not thick or fluffy, which allows water to dry quickly after swimming. The fur provides some protection from sun exposure but offers little insulation, which is why capybaras rely heavily on water and mud to regulate body temperature.

Their skin is thick and tough, helping protect them from bites, scratches, and environmental hazards. Capybaras often roll in mud, which acts as a natural sunscreen and insect repellent.

Lack of a Tai

Unlike many mammals, capybaras have no visible tail. This feature reduces drag in water and prevents injury while moving through dense vegetation. The absence of a tail contributes to their smooth, streamlined shape.

Internal Anatomy

Internally, capybaras have a highly specialized digestive system designed for breaking down fibrous plant material. Their large stomach and complex intestinal system allow them to extract nutrients from grasses that many other animals cannot digest.

They also practice **coprophagy**, meaning they eat certain types of their own droppings to re-digest nutrients and maintain healthy gut bacteria. This behavior is essential for their survival and overall health.

Anatomy and Survival

Efficient swimming

Long hours of grazing

Group living

Predator avoidance

Every part of their body works together to allow capybaras to survive in environments that are constantly changing and often dangerous.

5. Size of the Capybara

The capybara is the **largest rodent in the world**, and its size plays a major role in its behavior, survival, and social structure. Unlike smaller rodents that rely on speed or hiding, capybaras depend on their large body size, group living, and access to water for protection.

Average Size and Length

Adult capybaras typically measure **3.3 to 4.3 feet (1 to 1.3 meters)** in length from the head to the rear of the body. Their height at the shoulder usually ranges from **1.6 to 2 feet (50–60 centimeters)**. This makes them comparable in size to a medium-sized dog, though their body shape is much broader and heavier.

Their large, rounded bodies give them a powerful presence while still allowing them to move smoothly through water and vegetation.

Weight of Adult Capybaras

Fully grown capybaras usually weigh between **75 and 150 pounds (34–68 kilograms)**. Some individuals, especially large males living in ideal conditions, may exceed this range.

Weight varies depending on:

Food availability
Season
Age
Sex
Overall health

During wet seasons, when food is abundant, capybaras often gain weight. In dry seasons, they may lose some body mass due to limited grazing areas.

Growth from Birth to Adulthood

Capybaras are born relatively large compared to many other mammals. Newborn pups weigh around **3 to 4 pounds (1.5–2 kilograms)** and are able to walk, swim, and graze shortly after birth.

Growth is rapid during the first year of life. Young capybaras depend on their mother's milk but also begin eating grass within days. By the time they are several months old, they already resemble smaller versions of adults.

Most capybaras reach near-adult size by **12 to 18 months**, although they may continue to fill out and gain muscle mass for several more years.

Size Differences Between Males and Females

Male capybaras are generally **larger and heavier** than females. Adult males develop a noticeable scent gland on the top of the snout, which becomes more prominent as they mature. This gland is used for communication and dominance signaling.

Females tend to have slightly slimmer bodies, though the difference is subtle. During pregnancy, females may appear larger due to carrying multiple pups.

Body Size and Social Rank Size plays an important role in capybara social structure. Larger individuals often hold higher ranks within the group, especially

among males. Dominant capybaras typically have better access to food, mates, and preferred resting areas.

However, aggression is rare. Even large capybaras rely more on posture and presence than physical conflict to establish dominance.

Size and Predator Defense

The large size of capybaras helps reduce the number of predators capable of attacking them. While young capybaras are vulnerable, adults are too large for many predators.

When threatened, their size combined with strong swimming ability allows them to escape quickly into water. A fully grown capybara is difficult to capture once submerged.

Size in Captivity vs. the Wild

Capybaras living in protected environments or captivity often grow larger than those in the wild. Consistent food supply, lack of predators, and stable conditions allow them to reach their maximum potential size.

In the wild, environmental stress and competition may limit growth, especially during droughts or periods of food scarcity.

Why Size Matters

The size of the capybara defines much of its lifestyle:

Enables group protection
Supports long grazing periods
Reduces predation risk
Helps regulate body temperature

Their large body, combined with calm behavior and social cooperation, makes capybaras one of the most successful herbivores in South American ecosystems.

6. Eating Habits of the Capybara

Capybaras are **strict herbivores**, meaning their diet consists entirely of plant material. Their eating habits are closely connected to their habitat, social structure, and digestive system. As large grazing mammals, capybaras spend a significant portion of their day feeding in order to meet their nutritional needs.

Primary Diet

The main food source for capybaras is **grass**. They prefer soft, nutrient-rich grasses found near water sources such as riverbanks, wetlands, and floodplains. These grasses are abundant and regrow quickly, making them a reliable food supply for large groups.

In addition to grass, capybaras also eat:

Aquatic plants
Reeds and sedges
Leaves and shrubs
Bark and fruit (occasionally)

Their diet may change slightly depending on the season and availability of vegetation.

Grazing Behavior

Capybaras are **selective grazers**. Rather than eating plants randomly, they choose specific grasses that are easier to digest and richer in nutrients. They often graze during early morning and late afternoon when temperatures are cooler.

Grazing usually takes place in open areas near water. This allows capybaras to quickly escape into the water if predators appear. While feeding, at least one group member remains alert, watching for danger.

Seasonal Feeding Changes

During the wet season, food is abundant, and capybaras have access to a wide variety of grasses and aquatic plants. In the dry season, when water levels drop and vegetation becomes scarce, capybaras may travel farther to find food.

In dry conditions, they may rely more heavily on tougher plants, bark, or reeds. These foods are harder to digest but help sustain them until conditions improve.

Digestive System Adaptations

Capybaras have a **highly specialized digestive system** designed to break down fibrous plant material. Their large stomach and extended intestines allow bacteria to ferment cellulose, which is difficult for most animals to digest.

This fermentation process provides nutrients that would otherwise be unavailable. Because grass is low in energy, capybaras must eat large quantities to meet their nutritional needs.

Coprophagy (Re-Eating Droppings)

One of the most important aspects of capybara eating habits is **coprophagy**. This behavior involves eating specific types of their own droppings, usually soft pellets produced during digestion.

By doing this, capybaras:

Absorb additional nutrients
Maintain healthy gut bacteria
Improve digestion efficiency

This behavior is essential for survival and is common among herbivorous rodents.

Water and Feeding

Water plays a vital role in capybara feeding habits. Many of the plants they consume grow in or near water. Capybaras may feed on aquatic vegetation while partially submerged, which helps them stay cool and hidden from predators.

Water also supports digestion by helping regulate body temperature and maintaining overall health.

Group Feeding Dynamics

Capybaras usually feed in groups. Group feeding:

- Increases safety
- Reduces individual stress
- Allows young animals to learn feeding habits

Dominant individuals may choose the best grazing areas, but aggression over food is rare. Capybaras are generally tolerant and cooperative while feeding.

Feeding and Ecosystem Impact

By grazing continuously, capybaras help control plant growth and maintain healthy grasslands. Their feeding behavior:

Prevents overgrowth
Encourages plant regeneration

Supports biodiversity

They play an important ecological role as both consumers and prey within their ecosystems.

Why Eating Habits Matter

The eating habits of capybaras shape nearly every part of their lives, including:

Daily movement patterns
Group size and structure
Habitat selection
Survival during seasonal changes

Their ability to efficiently process plant material allows them to thrive in environments where many other large mammals cannot.

7. Reproduction Cycle of the Capybara

The reproduction cycle of the capybara is closely tied to its environment, social structure, and seasonal changes. As highly social mammals, capybaras reproduce in a way that supports group stability, protection of young, and long-term survival of the population.

Sexual Maturity

Capybaras reach sexual maturity relatively early for a large mammal.

Females usually become sexually mature between **12 and 15 months** of age.

Males typically mature slightly later, around **15 to 18 months**.

Although they may be physically capable of reproducing at this age, successful breeding often depends on social rank within the group, especially for males.

Seasonal Influence on Reproduction

The reproduction cycle of capybaras is strongly influenced by **seasonal rainfall**. Breeding activity increases during the **rainy season**, when food and water are abundant. These favorable conditions ensure that pregnant females have access to enough nutrition and that newborns are born during times of plenty.

During dry seasons, reproduction slows as resources become scarce. This natural timing improves survival rates for both mothers and offspring.

Estrous Cycle in Females

Female capybaras experience an estrous cycle, which is the period when they are receptive to mating. This cycle occurs regularly throughout the year but is more active during favorable environmental conditions.

When a female enters estrus, her behavior changes slightly. She may become more tolerant of male attention and remain closer to dominant males within the group. Chemical signals and subtle vocalizations also play a role in attracting mates.

Role of Dominant Males

In capybara groups, reproduction is often controlled by a **dominant male**. This male typically has priority access to females and fathers most of the offspring within the group. Dominance is established through size, confidence, and scent marking rather than frequent aggression.

Subordinate males may attempt to mate, but their success is limited. This social structure helps maintain order within the group and reduces conflict.

Mating Behavior

Mating usually takes place **in water**, which provides stability and safety. Water also helps support the female's body and reduces stress during mating. This behavior highlights the capybara's strong connection to aquatic environments.

Mating events are generally brief and may occur multiple times during a female's receptive period to increase the chances of successful fertilization.

Gestation Period

After successful mating, the female undergoes a **gestation period of about 150 days** (approximately five months). During pregnancy, females continue grazing and participating in group activities, though they may rest more frequently as birth approaches.

The long gestation period allows the young to develop fully before birth, increasing their chances of survival.

Birth and Litter Size

Capybaras give birth to **litters of 2 to 8 pups**, with an average of 4. Births usually occur on land, in sheltered areas close to water. Unlike many mammals, capybara pups are born:

Fully furred
With eyes open
Able to walk and swim shortly after birth

This advanced development allows them to keep up with the group almost immediately.

Care of the Young

Although the mother provides milk, young capybaras begin eating grass within a few days. Nursing continues for several weeks, but the pups gradually rely more on solid food.

One unique feature of capybara reproduction is **shared care**. Females within the group often help watch over and protect all the young, not just their own offspring. This cooperative behavior greatly improves survival rates.

Reproductive Success and Survival

The reproduction cycle of the capybara is highly efficient. By timing births with favorable seasons, producing well-developed young, and relying on group protection, capybaras ensure steady population growth under stable conditions.

This reproductive strategy reflects their social nature and adaptability, allowing them to thrive in challenging environments.

8. Breeding of the Capybara

Breeding in capybaras is a carefully coordinated process shaped by social hierarchy, environmental conditions, and strong group cooperation. Unlike solitary mammals, capybaras breed within stable social groups, where behavior, timing, and group dynamics all influence reproductive success.

Social Structure and Breeding Rights

Capybara groups usually consist of several adult females, their young, subordinate males, and one dominant male. This dominant male plays a central role in breeding. He establishes his status
through size, confidence, scent marking, and calm authority rather
than constant fighting.

Because of this hierarchy, the dominant male typically mates with most receptive females in the group. This system reduces conflict and creates stability, ensuring that breeding occurs without disrupting group cohesion.

Courtship Behavior

Capybara courtship is subtle and non-aggressive. When a female is ready to mate, she becomes more tolerant of the dominant male's presence. Courtship behaviors may include:

Following closely
Gentle nudging
Vocal communication such as soft whistles or clicks

There is no elaborate display. Instead, breeding relies on familiarity, social bonds, and timing.

Breeding in Water

One of the most distinctive features of capybara breeding is that **mating usually occurs in water**. Shallow water provides physical support for the female and allows both animals to remain balanced and calm.

Water also offers protection from predators and reduces stress, which increases the likelihood of successful mating. This behavior highlights how deeply breeding is connected to the capybara's semi-aquatic lifestyle.

Frequency of Breeding

Capybaras can breed **once or twice a year**, depending on environmental conditions. In areas with consistent rainfall and abundant food, females may reproduce more frequently.

Breeding frequency is closely linked to:

Food availability
Water levels
Overall group health

When conditions are poor, breeding naturally slows or pauses, conserving energy and resources.

Female Choice and Group Stability

Although the dominant male has priority, females are not forced to mate. Female choice plays an important role, as stressed or unhealthy females are less likely to reproduce successfully.

This balance between dominance and choice helps ensure healthier offspring and reduces unnecessary conflict within the group.

Breeding and Group Cooperation

Breeding is not just an individual event; it affects the entire group. Once females become pregnant, group behavior adjusts to support them. The group may:

Move more slowly Stay closer to water Remain more alert to predators

This cooperation improves survival chances for both mothers and unborn pups.

Breeding Success and Survival

Capybara breeding strategies are highly effective. By combining:

Social hierarchy
Environmental timing
Water-based mating
Group cooperation

capybaras maximize reproductive success while minimizing risk.

This system has allowed capybaras to maintain strong populations across large regions of South America, even in environments with predators and seasonal challenges.

Importance of Breeding Behavior

Breeding behavior reflects the core traits of capybaras:

Calm temperament
Social intelligence
Strong environmental awareness

Their breeding system is a key reason capybaras remain one of the most successful large herbivores in their natural habitats.

9. Growth of the Capybara

The growth of the capybara is steady, well-structured, and closely connected to nutrition, environment, and social support. From birth to full adulthood, capybaras develop rapidly compared to many mammals, allowing them to survive early life in environments where predators are common.

Birth and Early Development

Capybara pups are born highly developed. At birth, they:

Are fully furred
Have open eyes
Can walk and swim within hours
Weigh approximately **3–4 pounds (1.5–2 kg)**

This advanced development is critical for survival, as pups must keep up with the group almost immediately.

Within the first few days, young capybaras begin tasting grass, although they still rely heavily on their mother's milk.

Infancy Stage

During the first few weeks of life, growth is rapid. Pups nurse frequently and stay close to their mother or other adult females. One unique feature of capybara growth is **communal care**. Females in the group often watch over multiple pups, not just their own.

This shared protection:

Reduces stress on mothers
Protects pups from predators
Improves survival rates

During this stage, pups grow stronger legs, improved coordination, and increased swimming ability.

Juvenile Growth Phase

Between **2 and 6 months of age**, capybaras enter the juvenile stage. Milk intake decreases while grass consumption increases significantly. Their digestive system adapts to a fully herbivorous diet.

During this phase:

Body size increases rapidly
Muscle mass develops
Social behaviors become more noticeable

Young capybaras begin learning group rules, communication sounds, and safe feeding locations by observing adults.

Adolescent Development

From **6 months to 1 year**, capybaras resemble smaller adults. Their growth continues steadily, though at a slower pace than infancy. Bones strengthen, teeth continue developing, and body proportions become more balanced.

Adolescents may explore more independently but still remain close to the group. This period is essential for learning predator awareness and social rank positioning.

Reaching Adult Size

Most capybaras reach near-adult size between **12 and 18 months**. However, full physical maturity, including muscle development and body mass, may take up to **2–3 years**.

Males often grow larger and heavier during this period, especially if they rise in social rank. Females may slow growth slightly once they begin reproducing.

Factors Affecting Growth

Several factors influence how large and healthy a capybara becomes:

Food availability – consistent access to nutritious grass supports faster growth
Water access – essential for cooling, safety, and feeding
Group stability – reduced stress improves development
Environmental conditions – drought or habitat loss can slow growth

Capybaras raised in stable environments often reach their full growth potential.

Growth in the Wild vs. Protected Environments

In the wild, growth may slow during dry seasons or periods of food scarcity. In protected environments or captivity, capybaras often grow larger and more consistently due to steady nutrition and reduced threats.

However, even in the wild, their growth strategy is highly successful due to early independence and group support.

Why Growth Matters

Healthy growth is essential for:

Reducing vulnerability to predators
Establishing social rank
Successful reproduction
Long-term survival

The growth pattern of the capybara reflects its evolutionary success as a large, social, semi-aquatic herbivore.

10. Population and Threats to Capybaras

Capybaras currently maintain **stable populations** across much of their natural range, but their long-term survival depends on environmental health, habitat availability, and human behavior. Understanding both population trends and threats helps explain why capybaras remain common in some areas while declining in others.

Current Population Status Capybaras are not considered endangered on a global scale. In many regions of South America, they are widespread and locally

abundant. Their ability to reproduce efficiently, live in groups, and adapt to changing environments has helped maintain strong population numbers.

However, population density varies greatly depending on:

Water availability
Habitat quality
Human activity
Seasonal conditions

In protected wetlands and river systems, capybara populations often thrive.

Natural Population Regulation

Capybara populations are naturally regulated by:

Predation
Seasonal food availability
Disease
Environmental changes

Predators such as jaguars, pumas, anacondas, and caimans help keep populations balanced. Young capybaras are especially vulnerable, while adults rely on size and water escape for protection.

Seasonal droughts can reduce food and water, leading to temporary population declines. When conditions improve, populations often recover quickly.

Habitat Loss
One of the most serious threats to capybaras is **habitat destruction**. Wetlands, rivers, and floodplains are increasingly affected by:
Agriculture expansion
Urban development
Dam construction
Water diversion

When wetlands are drained or polluted, capybaras lose access to essential resources. Without nearby water, they cannot regulate body temperature, escape predators, or reproduce successfully.

Human-Wildlife Conflict

As capybaras adapt to human-modified environments, conflicts can occur. In agricultural areas, capybaras may graze on crops, leading farmers to view them as pests.

This conflict can result in:

Hunting
Relocation
Habitat removal

In some regions, road construction near water sources has increased vehicle collisions involving capybaras, especially during seasonal migrations.

Hunting and Exploitation

Capybaras are hunted in certain areas for their meat and skin. While controlled hunting may be sustainable in some regions, **overhunting** can reduce local populations if not properly managed.

Illegal hunting poses a greater threat, especially where enforcement is weak. Excessive hunting pressure can disrupt social groups and reduce reproductive success.

Climate Change Effects

Climate change presents an increasing long-term threat. Changes

in rainfall patterns can lead to:
Extended droughts
Reduced wetland areas
Altered vegetation growth

These changes affect food availability and water access, making survival more difficult in some regions.

Disease and Health Risks

High population density during dry seasons can increase the spread of disease. When many capybaras gather around limited water sources, parasites and infections can spread more easily.

Environmental pollution also weakens immune systems, making capybaras more vulnerable to illness.

Conservation and Protection

Capybaras benefit indirectly from wetland conservation programs. Protecting rivers, lakes, and floodplains helps preserve entire ecosystems, including capybaras.

In some areas, capybaras are protected by law, and sustainable management practices help balance human needs with wildlife conservation.

Why Population Awareness Matters

Monitoring capybara populations helps scientists:

Track ecosystem health
Identify environmental damage early
Develop conservation strategies

Because capybaras rely heavily on wetlands, their population trends often reflect the condition of freshwater ecosystems.

11. Social Structure of the Capybara

Capybaras are among the most **social mammals** in the animal kingdom. Their survival, reproduction, and daily activities depend heavily on living in organized groups. This strong social structure helps protect individuals from predators, improves access to resources, and supports the raising of young.

Group Size and Composition

Capybaras typically live in groups ranging from **10 to 20 individuals**, though groups may be smaller or much larger depending on environmental conditions. During dry seasons, when water sources are limited, groups may merge and form herds of **50 or more capybaras**.

A typical group includes:

One dominant adult male
Several adult females
Juveniles and pups
One or more subordinate males

This structure allows for stability, cooperation, and clear social roles.

Dominant Male Leadership

Each group is usually led by a **dominant male**, who plays a key role in maintaining order. He establishes his position through size, confidence, scent marking, and calm authority rather than frequent fighting.

The dominant male:

Protects the group
Controls breeding access
Marks territory
Responds first to threats

Aggression is rare, as dominance is usually respected once established.

Role of Females

Female capybaras form the social core of the group. They maintain close bonds with one another and play a major role in group stability. Females often cooperate in caring for young, watching over pups, and guiding group movement.

This cooperative behavior strengthens group unity and increases survival rates for offspring.

Subordinate Males

Subordinate males remain within the group but have lower social status. They may help watch for predators and participate in group activities but typically have limited access to breeding opportunities.

Some subordinate males eventually leave to form new groups or challenge other males when conditions allow.

Communication Within the Group

Capybaras communicate using a wide range of sounds, body language, and scent marking. Common vocalizations include:

Whistles
Barks
Clicks
Purr-like sounds

These signals are used to:

Warn of danger
Call group members
Maintain contact between adults and young

Scent marking, especially by dominant males, helps define territory and social status.

Group Movement and Cooperation

Groups move together when grazing, resting, or traveling between water sources. While feeding, some individuals remain alert, acting as lookouts while others graze. This shared vigilance reduces the risk of surprise attacks by predators.

When danger appears, the group often moves quickly and calmly toward water, demonstrating strong coordination.

Conflict Resolution

Conflict within capybara groups is minimal. When disagreements occur, they are usually resolved through posture, vocal signals, or avoidance rather than physical fights. This low-aggression social system helps prevent injury and maintains long-term group stability.
Benefits of Social Living

Living in groups provides many advantages:

Increased predator detection Protection of young Shared knowledge of food and water sources Reduced stress

Social living is one of the main reasons capybaras are so successful in challenging environments.

Why Social Structure Is Essential

The social structure of the capybara is not optional — it is essential for survival. Group living allows capybaras to thrive in habitats filled with predators, seasonal changes, and competition for resources. Their calm, cooperative nature makes them a powerful example of how social behavior can enhance survival in the wild.

12. Relationship Between Capybaras and Humans

The relationship between capybaras and humans is complex and varies widely depending on location, culture, and environmental conditions. In some regions, capybaras are valued and protected, while in others they are viewed as pests or resources. This relationship continues to evolve as human populations expand into natural habitats.

Historical Relationship

For centuries, indigenous communities in South America have lived alongside capybaras. These animals were traditionally hunted for food and materials, but hunting was usually small-scale and sustainable.

Capybaras were respected as part of the natural ecosystem, and their behavior, movements, and seasonal patterns were well understood by local people.

Capybaras as a Food Source

In some regions, capybaras are still hunted for their meat, which is considered a traditional food. Their meat is especially consumed during certain cultural or religious periods.

When hunting is:

Regulated and controlled, populations remain stable
Unregulated or illegal, local populations can decline

Sustainable management is essential to prevent overexploitation.Capybaras in Modern Human Environments

Capybaras are highly adaptable and increasingly live near:

Farms
Urban parks
Golf courses
Artificial lakes and reservoirs

These environments often provide abundant grass and water, allowing capybaras to thrive. However, close contact with humans can also create problems.

Human-Wildlife Conflict As capybaras move into human-dominated landscapes, conflicts may occur. Common issues include:

Crop damage
Competition with livestock
Road accidents near water sources

In agricultural areas, farmers may view capybaras as pests, leading to attempts to remove or control populations.

Capybaras as Pests vs. Protected Animals
In some countries, capybaras are legally protected, especially in national parks and conservation areas. In other regions, population control measures are allowed to reduce conflict.

The challenge is finding a balance between:

Protecting wildlife
Supporting human livelihoods
Preserving ecosystems

Poorly managed control efforts can disrupt social groups and increase stress and disease.

Capybaras and Ecotourism

Capybaras are popular with tourists due to their calm nature and social behavior. Wildlife viewing and ecotourism provide economic incentives to protect habitats and reduce hunting.

Their presence in natural parks often attracts visitors interested in observing:

Group behavior
Interaction with other animals
Semi-aquatic lifestyles

Ecotourism can promote conservation when managed responsibly.

Capybaras in Captivity and as Pets

In some places, capybaras are kept in zoos, wildlife parks, or private facilities. While they can become accustomed to human presence, capybaras are **not suitable pets** for most people.

They require:

Large spaces
Constant access to water
Social companionship
Specialized diets

Keeping them improperly can lead to stress, health problems, and behavioral issues.

Disease and Public Health Concerns

Close contact between capybaras, livestock, and humans can increase the risk of disease transmission. Capybaras may carry parasites or ticks that can affect other animals.

Proper habitat management and monitoring help reduce these risks while allowing coexistence.

Conservation and Coexistence

The future of the human-capybara relationship depends on responsible land use and conservation planning. Protecting wetlands, managing populations humanely, and educating communities are key steps.

Capybaras serve as an important reminder that:

Human actions directly affect wildlife Healthy ecosystems benefit both animals and people Coexistence is possible with thoughtful management Why the Human Relationship Matters

The way humans treat capybaras reflects broader attitudes toward nature. Because capybaras are adaptable and visible, they often become symbols of the challenges and opportunities involved in living alongside wildlife.

Their story highlights the importance of balance between development and conservation.

Thanks for reading facts about [animal name]. I am a parent of two boys on the autism spectrum. I am always advocating for Autism Spectrum Disorders which part of the proceeds of this book goes to many Non-Profit Autism Organizations. I would love if you would leave a review.

Author Note from Isis Gaillard:

Thanks For Reading! I hope you enjoyed the fact book about Capybaras

Please check out all the Learn With Facts series available.

Visit www.IsisGaillard.com and www.LearnWithFacts.com to find more books in the Learn With Facts Series

More Books In The Series

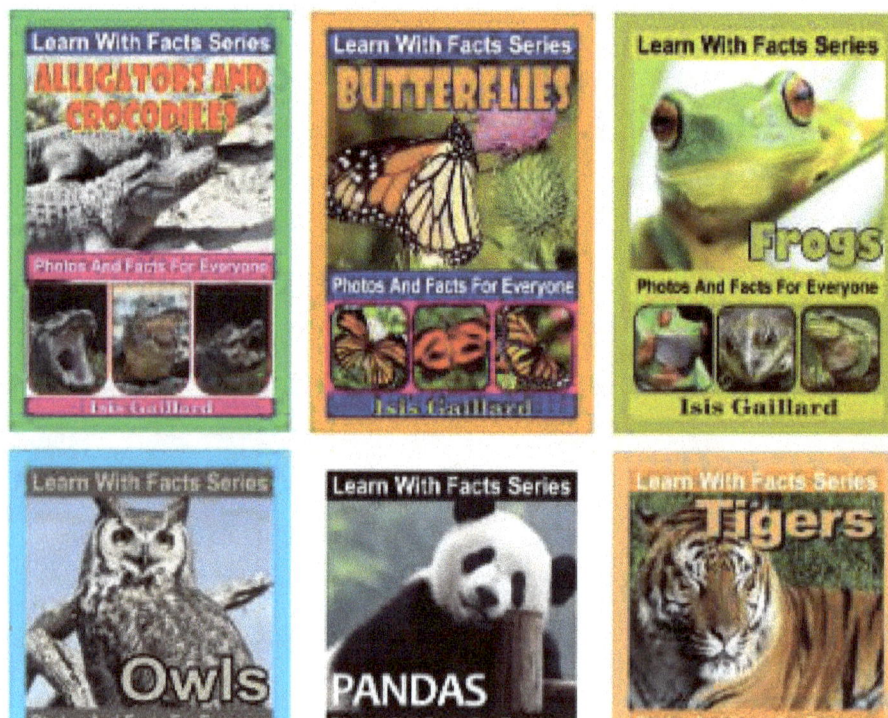

Over 170 books in the Learn With Facts Series.

www.ingramcontent.com/pod-product-compliance
Lightning Source LLC
Chambersburg PA
CBHW081421270326
41931CB00015B/3361